Between the Sky and Floor

more poems and drawings by
Mr. Huie

Copyright © 2001
Keith Huie/Jingle Books
PO Box 457
Sun Prairie, WI 53590

Library of Congress Control #: 2001126607

ISBN: 0-9710041-0-2

First printing: June 2001
Second printing: June 2003

Printed in the USA by Morris Publishing
3212 East Highway 30, Kearney, NE 68847
800-650-7888

Other books by Mr. Huie:

Bed Skulls
poems and drawings

Captain Everybody
still more poems and drawings

For Dad,
Creator of the Purple Sleeping Bag Monster

Confidence In, Confidence Out

Confidence in
Confidence out
Just go and do it
There's no need to shout
Like it or not
Give it your best
Believe in yourself
Life has its tests

The Kid Who Made Up Words

The kid who made up words
Was told to go chop wood.
All he said was, "Farpemloop."
And no one understood.
The kid who made up words
Bit bananas that were bruised.
All he said was, "Gorgonding."
And people looked confused.
The kid who made up words
Was climbing on some boulders.
At the top, he yelled, "Kashlop!"
And people shrugged their shoulders.
The kid who made up words
Was eaten by a trout.
Down in the fish, he shouted, "Help!"
And the people pulled him out.

3

4

Big Jim Timber

Big Jim Timber?
Lumberjack.
Knocks down trees?
Just one whack.
Clears a forest?
Day and a half.
Shakes the ground?
When he laughs.
Flannel shirt?
Red and green.
Is it dirty?
Keeps it clean.
Ax or saw?
Uses both.
Bearded chin?
Facial growth.

Courage

I've been to the edge but never jumped.
I've sat in the dark and seen the light.
I've wanted to quit and persevered.
I've lost many battles and continued to fight.

Plus or Minus?

Are you a plus or minus?
Are you honest or amiss?
Pro or con?
Right or wrong?
Just or devious?
Corrupt and cruel and foul?
Noble, true and fair?
Are you a plus or minus?
Do you tear down or repair?

Going With the Flow

I was having a meal of meat
When a vegetarian took a seat.
Though we talked and disagreed,
I went out back and killed a tree.
I fed the tree to my veggie guest
And was soon confronted by a naturalist,
Who was highly offended by the tree's demise,
So I planted a seed to compromise.
A wonderful meal, a guest list twist,
Meat and veggies and a naturalist.

9

Shoot Bang

Shoot Bang was a cowboy.
He was long, thin, lean and tall.
He owned one hundred cowboy hats,
And he liked to wear them all.
Every morning when he woke
He would try to ride his horse,
But wearing all one hundred hats,
It was very hard of course.
Shoot Bang knew the thing to do
Was to buy another steed.
"One will carry my hats," he said.
"And the other will carry me."

11

Weather or Not

Thunder sounds like a parade is coming.
Lightning is a picture just taken.
Wind feels like an invisible hand.
Rain is sizzling bacon.

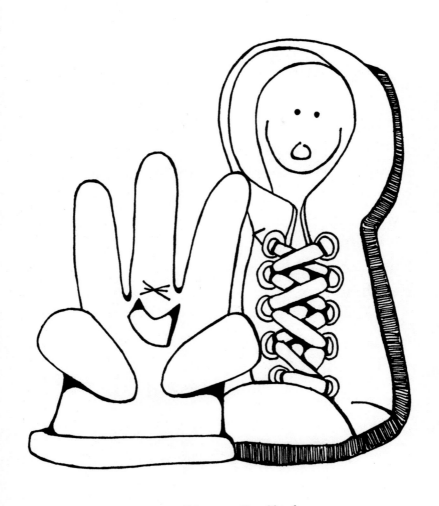

My Shoes Smiled

You tickled me so hard, my shoes smiled!
And my hat grinned ear to ear!
My socks and mittens lost their breath!
And my pants cried happy tears!

13

I Wish They Would

I wish that homework did itself.
I wish lost things jumped out.
I wish last picked was considered best.
I wish that secrets would shout.
I wish that insults whispered.
I wish hurt feelings showed.
I wish that dark were lighter.
I wish all monsters glowed.

50/50

Have you been to the park?
Have you seen the snow?
Have you climbed the hill
Where the sledders go?
Have you sat in your sled?
Have you stared at the ice?
Have you wanted to leave?
Have you thought twice?
Have you watched the winter's day
Turn slowly into night?
Do you feel the chilling wind?
Is your scarf and cap on tight?
Are you holding on to the rope?
Has the snot froze to your nose?
Are you ready for disaster?.....
...Or success,....who knows?

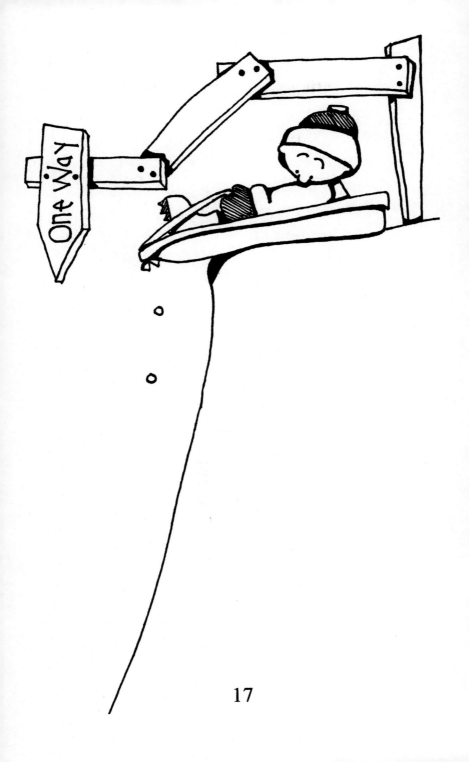

Just South of Canada

Mondovi, Potosi, Viroqua, Ozaukee,
Tomah, Iola, Menasha, Pewaukee,
Monroe, Wautoma, Waupaca, Milwaukee,
Wausau, Minocqua, Juneau, Wausaukee,
Outagamie, Monticello,
Wauwatosa, Lac du Flambeau,
Waukesha, Waterloo,
Oconomowoc, Baraboo,
Weyauwega, Manitowoc,
Kenosha, Wautoma, Wonewoc,
Tripoli, Okauchee, Waunakee,
Kewaunee, Pulaski, Menominee,
Antigo, De Soto, Mukwonago,
Muskego, Monona and Buffalo.

Nowhere Near the End

Has anyone seen Mark McConville?
I heard he never came home.
Does anyone know where he might be?
Did someone leave him alone?
I hope you know what this means.
We've lost another friend.
No more going anywhere alone.
We're nowhere near the end.

19

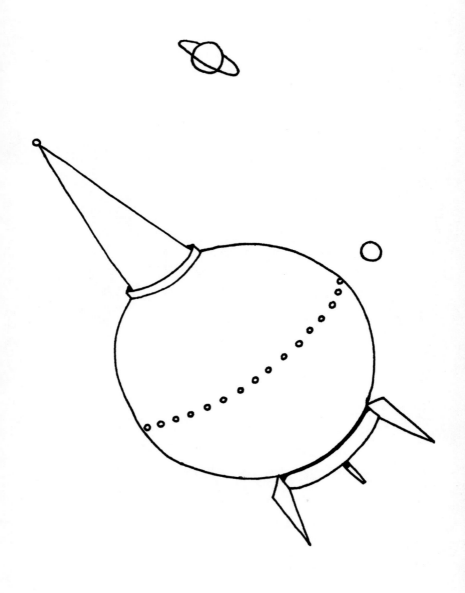

20

Earth Remembered

I've seen trees in old time photos.
I've seen rocks at the museum.
The old people talk about shapes in the clouds.
What are clouds? I've never seen 'em.
I've heard about food that grew on trees.
They called it bananas? Or apples? Or peas?
Everything I eat is processed until
It fits in a three course, vitamin pill.
My grandparents went out to play in........snow?
We don't leave the ship. There's nowhere to go.
Most every day, my friends and I play
In the thrust reactor core's nonhazardous spray.
My forefathers orbited around the sun.
I float on a ship through space.
I don't remember my ancestor's world.
But it sounds like a very odd place.

The Olson Octuplets

The Olson octuplets were born today,
1 blue, 1 red, 4 green, 2 gray.
The Olson octuplets, all very cute,
2 boys, 3 girls, 2 cats and a boot.
The Olson octuplets, different all,
4 big, 1 short and 3 very small.
The Olson octuplets have special names,
1 Percy, 3 Marcy, 3 Francis, 1 James.
The Olson octuplets sleep in one bed,
1 blanket, 1 pillow, no teddies, 1 spread.
The Olson octuplets, each one unique,
All strong, all brave, all funny, all meek.

Pimpster Flimpster

Pimpster Flimpster dug a hole
With a pick, a shovel and a fishing pole.
The pick broke rock.
The shovel scooped dirt.
The fishing pole matched his favorite shirt.
Pimpster Flimpster picked and dug.
He happened upon a lamp and a rug.
The lamp was lethargic.
The rug was alert
And both looked good with his favorite shirt.
Pimpster Flimpster took a rest,
Laid on his back, not on his chest.
The nap felt good.
The rocks kind'a hurt
And put small holes in his favorite shirt.
Pimpster Flimpster climbed out of the ground
And was quite distressed by what he found.
His voice gave a cry.
His eyes gave a squirt.
Flimpster had ruined his favorite shirt.

Clueless

The last line of this poem is missing,
But I know it's still in the book.
Can you help me find it?
Will you please just take a look?
I know it's here, and very near,
I just don't know it's fate.
Look around, up and down,

Can She?

Can a girl be smart and pretty?
Can a girl be cool and brave?
Can a girl be more than just one thing?
Can she goof off and behave?
Can she acquiesce?
Can she be in charge?
Can she do what she wants to do?
Can she be both small and large?

The Good Life

I'm going to be a millionaire!
There is a place I've found
Where chocolate raisins turn to dimes
When you drop them on the ground!
Sweet, delicious, dried up grapes!
Covered in chocolate to spare!
There's enough to fill my bank!
But not enough to share!

The Lying Game

At this game I am the worst,
'cause when I lie, my stomach hurts,
And my throat gets a lump,
And my hands start to sweat.
I'll always lose this game I bet.

29

Squeaky Spindle

I spin a squeaky spindle
Underneath the springy stars.
Blue Apaches on fuzzy horses,
Crimson cowboys play cotton guitars.
The lion and grizzly are by my side,
Suspended between the sky and floor.
We bounce and rock and whisper talk,
Watching for dad at my bedroom door.

Who Am I?

What is it about this voice of mine
That makes me so unique?
What makes me so different
From others that I meet?
There are millions of people in the world
Who all have voices too.
What makes me so special?
What makes me something new?
Are my thoughts that special?
Is my life a wonderful gift?
Can I change the world around me?
Can I give mankind a lift?

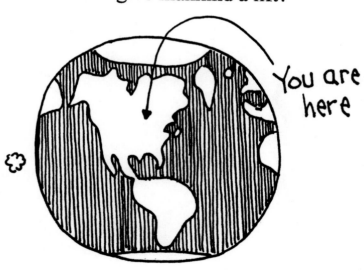

You are here

Chicago

Do you see the boy outside the window
Without his mom or dad?
He doesn't really look too happy,
But he doesn't look too sad.
Should I sit and just ignore him,
And turn my head away?
Or go out on the Chicago streets
And see if he's okay?

33

Acquaintances

Why did the chicken cross the road?
To save the hamster from the toad.
Why was the toad so agitated?
He thought the hamster was someone he hated.
Why did the chicken get involved?
To help them get their problems solved.
How did he show them something new?
Common ground and speaking true.
Did they all become fast friends?
No, but hatred came to an end.

35

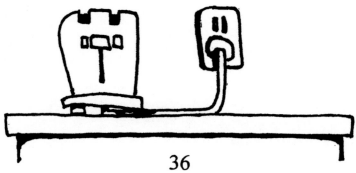

Overcrowding

It seems to me
As I walk along
Past the cupboard door,
More people are here
Up on the shelves
Than there's ever been before.
A very nice family
Moved in last night.
They live in the cereal bowls,
Next to the Johnsons,
Who live in the strainer.
Their feet get stuck in the holes.
The top shelf
Used to be deserted,
A place for me to play.
But now it's packed
From the mugs that are cracked
All the way down to the tray.
It's crowded here in the cupboard
And the numbers continue to grow.
But I'll stay with the masses,
Here with the glasses,
'cause it's the only home I know

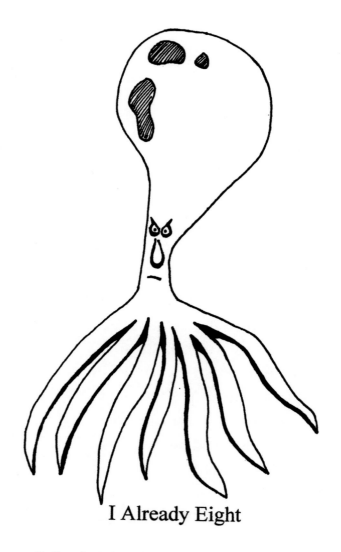

I Already Eight

I don't eat octopus..........it's true.
I don't like octopus..........do you?
I don't eat octopus..........you do?!
I don't like octopus..........or you.

Gargoyle

Concrete grin
Marble eyes
Granite fingers
Watch the skies
Crooked teeth
Limestone ears
Pointed nose
Frozen years

The Spider's Hall of Heroes

Little Leah spotted a spider
Sitting in a web with her babies beside her.
She spared the young
And that's why she's hung
In the Spider's Hall of Heroes.
Doug saw a spider on his bedroom floor.
He helped it out his home's back door.
Courageously conducted
And now he's inducted
In the Spider's Hall of Heroes.
Crystal came in and shouted, "Stop!"
"Don't smash spiders with brooms and mops!"
For defying the gang
She'll always hang
In the Spider's Hall of Heroes.
Take care of spiders, though they look scary,
And big and gross and creepy and hairy.
If you're loyal and true
There's a spot for you too
In the Spider's Hall of Heroes.

Confidence and Mischief

Slap a baby tornado.
Poke a shark right in the eyes.
Put a dog and cat together.
Win the biggest bowling prize.

Less Noise

Stop Talking!! That's what you need to
Hear. But your friends just can't
Unite.
Tragically, the people around you are

Usually
Polite

Flip-flop

Have you ever wanted back
The words that you have said?
Like "hate" or "jerk" or "idiot"?
Like "shut up" or "drop dead"?
You can ask for them politely
From the person that you gave 'em.
Just replace them with a new one
Like "sorry" or "forgiven?"

45

Two Cent Seltzer Water

"Two cent seltzer water!"
We heard the waiter bellow.
"Two cent seltzer water!
Can I find a daring fellow?
I'll buy your drink,"
He said with a wink.
"And I only have one rule.
After you slurp,
You cannot burp.
Who is ready for the duel?"
We raised our hands 100 times
On 100 separate trips,
And we never won,
But we did have fun,
As the burps rolled past our lips!

@#*!!

I slipped a piece of pizza in
And burned the roof of my mouth.
I pulled it out, and with a shout,
I let a @#*!! slip out.
Now I'm sitting in my room
While my family dines.
I wish that @#*!! hadn't slipped,
Then things would be just fine.

48

Compassion

Rest in peace stones
Dot the grass.
Cars drive slow.
I watch them pass.
Tinted windows
Cannot hide
The hopeless faces
That cry inside.

Feed the Mountain

Pile the rocks.
Stack the sticks.
Leave a present
Just for kicks.
Take a rake.
Smooth the bumps.
Collect the trash.
Remove the stumps.
Pull some grass,
A delicious blend,
And feed the mountain,
He's your friend.

The Ugly President

You are the captain
Of the stupid patrol.
The king of the snot drinking,
Raw sewage trolls.
The leader of the weirdoes
In the Kingdom of Nuts.
The ugly President
Of the United Butts.

Chocolate or Vanilla?

Chocolate or vanilla,
Which do you prefer?
If we choose to mix
These two picks,
Should a brand new name occur?
Vanocolate or chanilla,
Which do you prefer?
What new name
Should get the fame,
When we mix and stir?

53

Passing Around the Blueberry Goo

Passing around the blueberry goo,
From him to her to them to you.
Around the table, every place,
Take a drink, make a face.
It doesn't really look too good.
Everyone frowns. Do you think you should?
All at the table have had their drink.
Go on! Your turn! What do you think?

All of your friends are staring at you.
Do you take a drink of the blueberry goo?

56

Dead Fish

I like to stare at dead fish,
And cars that crash on the road,
Broken bones, but not my own,
And the ant covered, dried up toad.
I'm not sure why I look
At the nest that fell from the tree,
Or the bleeding cut
And the homeless mutt,
Something just fascinates me.
I don't go looking for gross things,
Or things most others find ill,
But I can't look away
When they are displayed,
And I don't think I ever will.

X's and O's

In math I got a hug.
In art I got a kiss.
In gym I held a friend's hand.
Can you imagine this?
What if school were fuzzy?
Would it ease your woes,
If instead of A's and B's
They gave out X's and O's?

Lemonade

If you ever break your leg,
Pretend your cast is a wooden peg.
Paint it brown up to your hip
And spend the day on a pirate ship.

Haiku

Difficult writing
Haiku stands 5,7,5
I don't understand

Dracula William Green

Someday when you have your kids,
Don't rest upon a shelf.
Show respect for the village,
But raise your kids yourself.

VCR

I watch movies in my head,
On my boat and in my car,
In school, at home and on the bus,
With my forehead VCR.

Effort

Work hard enough to sweat.
Get headaches when you think.
Play until your muscles hurt.
Get close enough to stink.

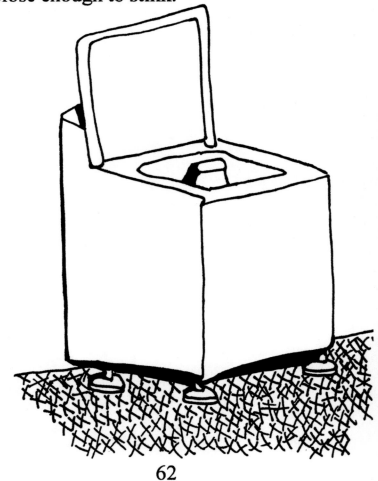

63

Ode to Easter

Easter bunny, Easter bonnet,
Easter basket with flowers on it.
Easter candy, Easter day,
Easter eggs hidden away.
Run through the grass!
Run through the woods!
Fill your basket
With Easter goods!
Jelly beans and marshmallow chicks!
Chocolate bunnies and peppermint sticks!
Eat sweets for breakfast!
Eat sweets for lunch!
Eat sweets for dinner!
Drink sweet Easter punch!
At bedtime things begin to change.
Suddenly, you're feeling strange.
Too much sugar, vision is blurring,
Irrational, hyper, your speech is slurring.
Up till eleven, you cannot sleep.
Too much candy. Too many sweets.
Soon your stomach starts to ache.
For the sink you make a break.

Up come the beans and marshmallow chicks!
Up come the bunnies and peppermint sticks!
Now your head is a ton of lead.
You cannot make it back to bed.
Passed out on the bathroom floor,
Easter is over, it's twelve o'four.

Sherry Loon

Sherry Loon
Jumped to the moon
And landed in a crater.
She thought she was alone
But she had landed in the home
Of a moon crater monster that ate her!

A Squirrels Life

Born
Grow
Summer
Snow
Run
Jump
Sit
Stump
Eat
Sleep
Wire
Creep
Car
Road
Squirrel
Nuts
Car
Screech
Squirrel
Guts

Trophy Brophy

Trophy Brophy
Won again.
Another trophy
For the den.
Trophy Brophy
Won the race.
He caught the ball.
He drew the ace.
He stopped the puck.
He beat the clock.
He kicked the point.
He threw the block.
He slid home safe.
He made the catch.
He sunk the shot.
He took the match.
He got the prize.
He hit the pitch.
He broke the tape.
He soaked the witch.
He scored the goal.
He came in first.
He is the best.
I am the worst.

69

Summer is an Hour Away

Summer is an hour away,
I can feel it in the air!
Summer is an hour away,
I get to buzz my hair!
Summer is an hour away,
I've got new shorts to wear!
Summer is over? It's time for school?
I don't think that's fair.

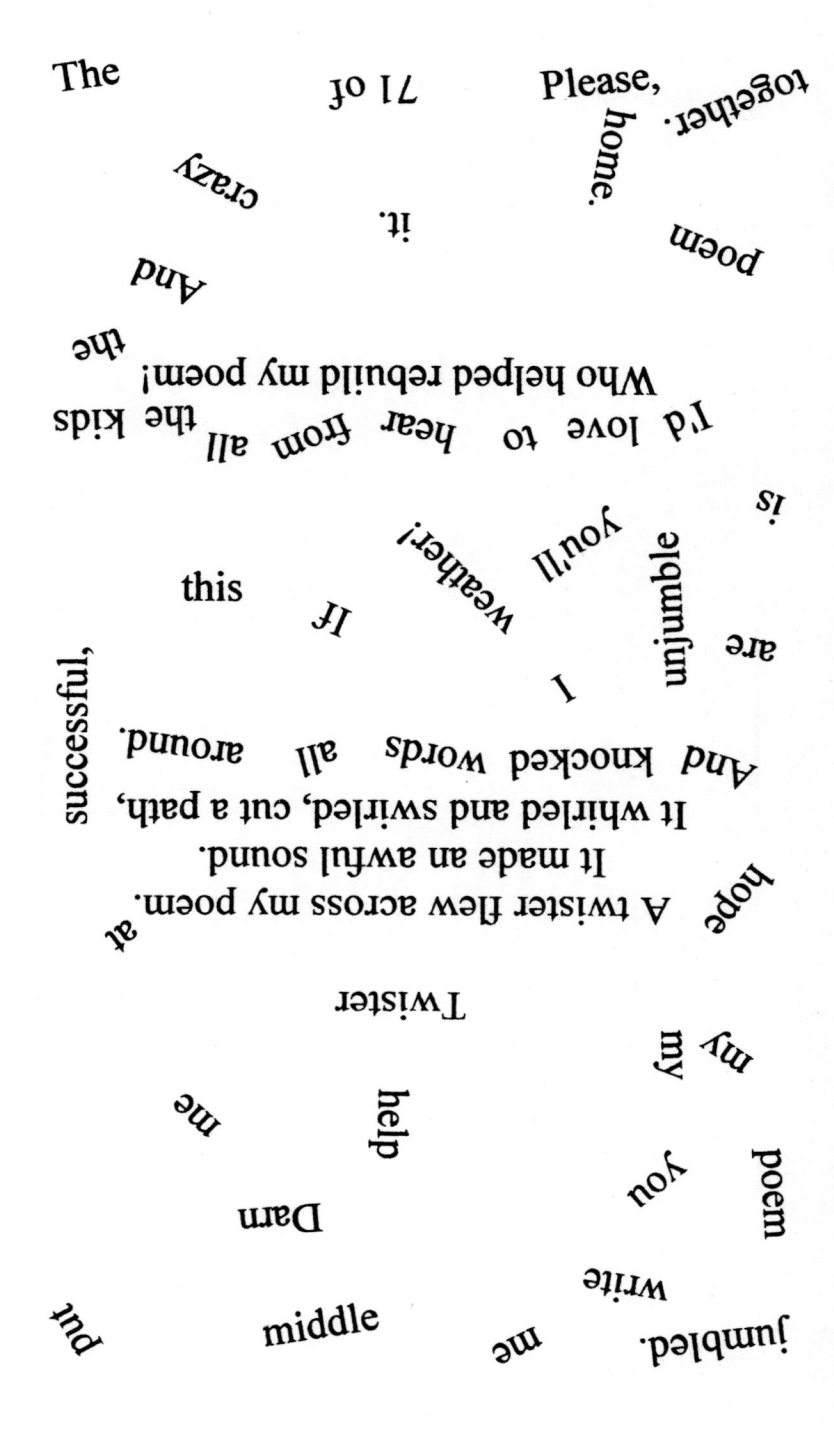

Wearing Shorts

I ran away today
Up inside my head.
Right in the middle of English,
I went outside instead.
I stood up in the classroom,
And walked right out of school.
That's me outside the window,
Bending one more rule.

72

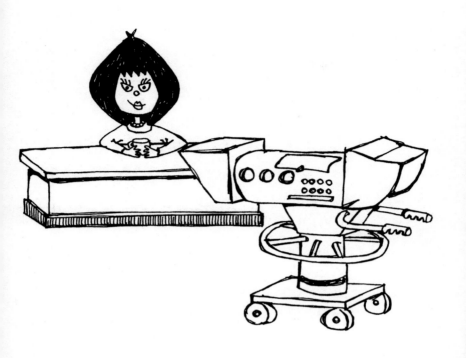

TV Katy

TV Katy reads and writes
The TV news both days and nights.
When I turn my TV on,
I always start to stretch and yawn,
If it's not TV Katy on.
But I will watch the news from Haiti,
Whether it be light or weighty.
I will watch until I'm eighty,
If it's read by TV Katy.

Seasons Greedings

"It's not the right color!"
"This is too small!"
"What were you thinking?!"
"I wanted a doll!"
"How much was this?!"
"Do you have the receipts?!"
"This doesn't seem fair!"
"They got more sweet treats!"
"He has more presents!"
"Her stack is taller!"
"It's not what I wanted!"
"Was this gift a dollar?!"
"I already have one!"
"This isn't enough!"
"I only got clothes!"
"I need some more stuff!"

People Fall Down

Wave your arms
Shake your head
Sing and dance
Raise the dead
Drool a bit
Twist and shout
Sit back down
The urge is out

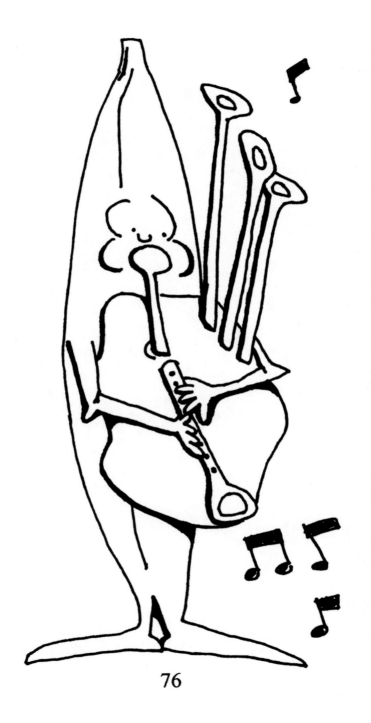

Fruisic

Banana played the bagpipes
Apple played the flute
Kiwi played the trumpet
Toot, toot, toot
Grape played the trombone
Orange played the drums
Peach played the cello
Hum, hum, hum
Cherry played
The tuba
Lemon played
The strings
Melon played
The hand bells
Ding, ding, ding

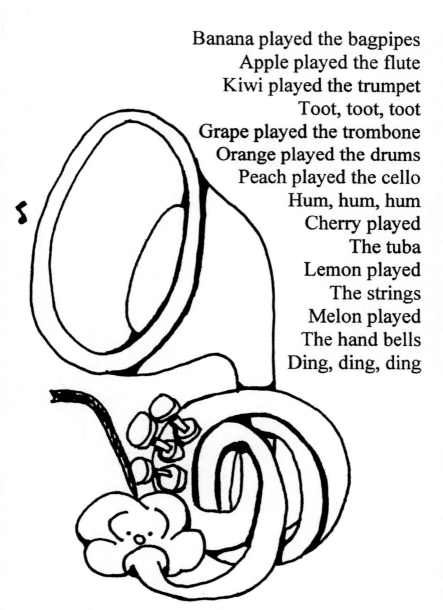

Cal Q. Later

Cal can add his toes and toys
And subtract that from the number of boys
In Miss O'Hagen's first grade class
And divide it by the number of bass
That swim out back in the pond in his yard
And multiply that by the number of cards
He got last year when he was sick
And add that to the number of bricks
It took to build his neighbors house
And multiply that by the one white mouse
That lives in the tree that is next to the fence
And subtract that from the number of dents
That are in the door of his father's car
And add that to the number of stars
He sees at night when he goes to bed
And he does it all up in his head.
My friend Cal is very bright,
And he always gets the answer right.

Things I Can Live Without

One kidney
One lung
One foot
Both ears
A nose
My toes
My hair
My tears
Appendix
Some teeth
My tonsils
And drool
Knuckles
Elbows
Homework
And school

MATH

TRASH

www.grandma@heaven.com

I hope that God has e-mail.
I hope that He's on line.
I miss my grandma very much,
And I hope she's doing fine.
My calls do nothing but ring all day,
And she won't return my faxes.
She left her pager here on earth
On the dresser with her taxes.
I hope God is watching the computer screen,
So I can reach my mother's mom.
I log on each day, and hope and pray,
www.grandma@heaven.com.

Tina Half Head

I met Tina Half Head
At a quarter after two.
Three fourths of the way down seventh street,
We ate a bowl of stew.

Thanks Dad

I tried to eat a beetle today
But my father told me, "No!"
He said, "Ick! It'll make you sick!"
So I let the beetle go.

83

Oops!

Sometimes I brim the tushes.
Sometimes I snovel show.
Sometimes I bead a rook,
Or watch some gowers flow.
Sometimes I fo gishing.
I like to catch wartoons.
Sometimes I wike lishing.
I like to mook at the loon.
Sometimes I flay pootball.
I like to nake a tap.
Sometimes I like to lim in a swake.
And wear my caseball bap.
When it comes to writing
I am really quite smart,
Each day I get better and better.
But sometimes when I sit down to write,
I still lix up the metters.

85

In The Pendant

It's fun to fit in with your friends.
It's fun when you look cool.
But what if your friends
Are acting dumb?
Do you want to be a fool?
If everyone has decided
To do something that's wrong.
There is not safety in numbers,
You can stay or go along.

Heads or Eagles?

Is it heads or eagles?
C'mon, let me see.
If it's heads, I win again.
How 'bout two out of three?

87

$1.00 a Jump!!

$1.00 a jump!!
$1.00 a jump!!
Get a fast running start
And land on your rump!
Summer to fall!
October, November!
Piles of leaves!
A treat to remember!
Orange and yellow!
Brown and red!

88

Nature's cast offs!
A crunchy bed!
Jump over a rope!
Jump through a hoop!
Wait! What's that smell!?
AAAAAAHHHH!! It's poop!!
Nickel a jump,
Nickel a jump,
Just be very careful,
The dog took a dump.

90

Ridzoooofal

I went into the grocery store.
The VP came with a liberal roar.
He took my food and ran out the door.
He screamed, "It's the will of the people!"
I chased him down a crooked street.
Following a trail of bread and meat.
I found him sitting in a comfortable seat.
He screamed, "It's the will of the people!"
He stuffed his face and got his fill,
Hiding behind the people's will.
I walked away, he was eating still.
He screamed, "It's the will of the people!"
The VP took a pompous drive,
Past the hungry and victimized.
Coyly wiping deceptive eyes,
Mocking the will of the people.

The Prairie School for the
Terminally Uncompliant

They built a school on the prairie
For the kids that wouldn't comply.
They emptied the schools of resistance,
So the gifted kids could fly.
Tommy was sent there. He's USL.
Unable to Stay in Line.
BeeBee was sent there. She's SHM.
She likes to Speak Her Mind.
Kevin is TC,
He Talks in Class.
Sam is CP,
She just Can't Pass.
Teddy is CT,
A Creative Thinker.
Brandon is LS,
A Little Stinker.
Megan is DD,
She won't Do Division.
Bryan, CMD,
He Can't Make Decisions.
Morgan is DC,

She Doesn't Conform.
Rayroy is RN,
Rejects the Norm.
All of these kids, creative and clever,
Are tough to figure out.
But these are the ones, daughters and sons,
Lore will be written about.

Things To Do

Cancel my space shuttle flight.
Study for my test.
Bounce in the middle of the trampoline.
Win a fish down at the fest.
Spend half of my allowance.
Pretend to brush my hair.
Return the movies we rented.
Pick out clothes to wear.
Fight aliens in my bedroom.
Sharpen pencils for school.
Read a book in fifteen minutes.
Get the leaves out of the pool.
Bring wood in from the backyard.
Make sure the dog is fed.
Help mom with the dishes.
Sail to Paris on my bed.

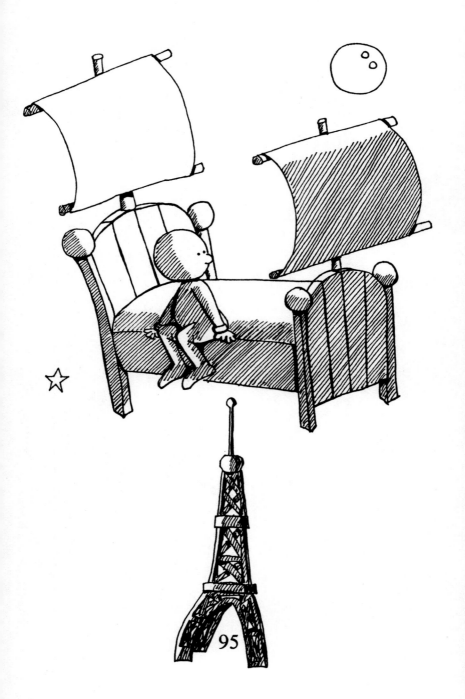

Patch

A pumpkin in a patch of mushrooms.
A giant among the weak,
Standing stoic, firm and heroic,
Protecting the fungi, small and meek.
The mushrooms huddle to him,
Protection from the cold.
They trust him completely, humbly and sweetly,
And hope he never grows old.
But the pumpkin knows the future,
He can feel the coming chills.
He prepares the 'shrooms for his ultimate doom,
Confidence instilled.

Common Sense

1+1 is always 2.
There's a thousand ways to draw a shoe.
2+2 is always 4.
There's a hundred ways to paint a door.
4+4 is always 8.
There's a million ways to chalk a slate.
8+8 is always......hmmmm?
I think I'll go draw.

97

My Christmas Tree

Flashing lights and silver balls,
My Christmas tree has got it all!
Pine cones and popcorn! Cranberries too!
Bells and elves and a star or two!
Socks and clocks and Jupiter rocks!
Gum and broken bicycle locks!
Licorice whips and pantyhose!
Ticket stubs from movie shows!
Pencils and pens and wooden spoons!
Forks and knives and big balloons!
Coffee cups and candy bars!
The rear view mirror from the family car!
Baseball cards and paper clips!
Football cleats and model ships!
Two of my sister's paper dolls!
A souvenir from Niagara Falls!
Reading glasses! Old tin cans!
Ornamental Chinese fans!
Mom's best jewelry! A burned out fuse!
The laces from my tennis shoes!
Silver dollars and dominoes!
A hundred foot, green garden hose!

Fishing reels and pocket knives!
Roller blades and honey bee hives!
Billiard balls and candle drips!
The rigging from a pirate ship!
Twenty five jars of volcanic ash!
AAAAAAAHHHHH! LOOK OUT! It's falling!
SMASH!

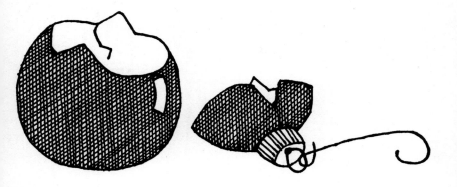

180 Degrees

I woke up this morning
And finally knew,
The dreams I have
Are coming true.
Because I listened
And did what was right
I have great days
And peaceful nights.
Every day is a new beginning,
A chance to start again.
To do my best,
To pass the test,
To be different than I've been.

100

Cool

Lighting matches on planes that fly overhead.
Safe and secure in a woodpecker's bed.
Searching the clouds for humorous shapes.
Snacking on seeds and wafers and grapes.
Hoping that the day won't end.
Bobbing as the branches bend.
Watching rain clouds fill the sky,
I use a leaf to keep me dry.

A Ghost Named Grindle

A ghost named Grindle
Spun his spindle
High in the castle
Of Watunda Watindle.
Spinning a thread
From the hair of the dead,
The dead of Watunda Watindle.
Life once kindled
Has long since dwindled.
The people are gone
From Watunda Watindle.
They all died from fright
When they got their first sight
Of the ghost of Watunda Watindle.

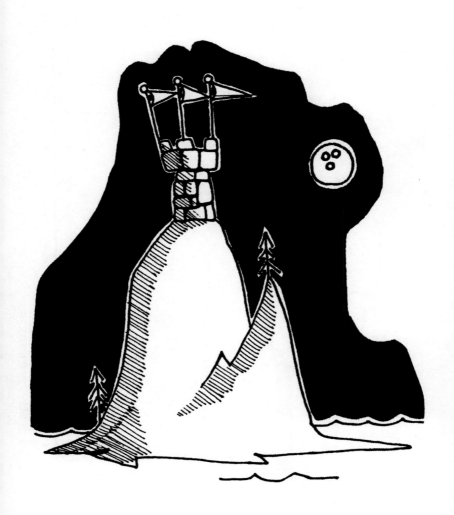

103

Don't Get Lost in Second Grade

They are going to tell you
To sit still and not talk
To raise your hand
To not throw sand
To hold hands when you walk
To share your things
But not your lunch
To take turns on the slide
To walk, not run
Do not play guns
To say the pledge with pride
But don't get lost in second grade
Find a way to glow
Jump and giggle
Wink and wiggle
Don't go with the flow
Put your heart into each day
Teach them something new
Show respect, but please protect
The stuff that makes you you

Good Luck

I opened my umbrella in the house
And a rabbit's foot flew out.
It cracked a mirror when it hit.
Now I'm filled with doubt.
Will my four leaf clover
Be enough to turn the tide?
Or, should I salt my shoulder
And turn and run and hide?

106

Lot 57, Westview Heights

Lot 57, Westview Heights,
Pine tree left, maple right.
Shutters and gables and windows and stairs,
A chimney and fire and smoky air.
Noises come from behind closed doors.
Yet, no one walks the dusty floors.
Ghosts are rumored to float inside,
But the doors are locked. I know, I tried.

Swordbirds

Birds with swords for noses,
Right outside the kitchen.
Drinking scarlet, sugar water,
A White Lake June tradition.
Just outside the window,
As the day begins anew,
Grandpa and me, toast and tea,
The swordbirds and the view.

Surrounded By Dogs In a Preacher's Bathroom
In the Middle of the Night

"Mom and dad!! Mom and dad!!
This stupid door won't open!"
I'm sure these dogs are friendly,
At least that's what I'm hopin'.

FDTD

From dad to daughter
I want to say,
Get up early
On Christmas day.
From dad to daughter
I want you to know,
Magic lives
In the falling snow.
From dad to daughter
I hope you can see,
There is always time
To climb a tree.
From dad to daughter
Take the time,
To write things down,
To sing and rhyme.
From dad to daughter
Don't be scared,
Speak your mind,
Be prepared.
From dad to daughter
Strong and proud,
Do what's right,
Defy the crowd.

Backwards Girl

Erin eats dinner for breakfast,
And breakfast comes at dinner.
She finished last in a running race,
And claimed to be the winner!
She arrives at school in the afternoon,
And leaves when the sun comes up.
She drinks her tea from a tennis shoe
And covers her feet with cups!
She likes to sleep on the television
And sit and watch her bed!
She keeps the canary in her hat,
Wears a birdhouse on her head!

111

The Pirate's Underwater Easter

An old, wooden ship, long ago sunk.
Cold, pirate ghosts asleep in their bunks,
Waking up early on Easter day,
To search for eggs in Antigo Bay.
Floating and bobbing, baskets in hand,
Hunting for treasure in the colorful sand.
Buccaneer corpses gleefully romp,
Darting along the ocean floor swamp.
Peg legs and hook hands cover the sea
Wondering where the booty might be.
Rotting cadavers of the seas evil crew
Celebrating Easter, kinda' like you.

No Man

I'd rather live without a car
Than have nowhere to go.
I'd rather live without a summer
Than never see the snow.
I'd rather live with a broken heart
Than never be in love.
I'd rather live with you in the depths
Than all alone above.

Old

Cannot climb the stairs
Losing all my hairs
Sit and wait and stare
No one seems to care

Pumpkin Dung

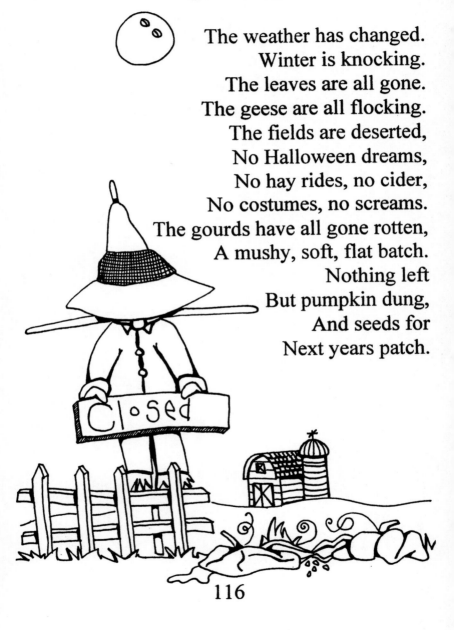

The weather has changed.
Winter is knocking.
The leaves are all gone.
The geese are all flocking.
The fields are deserted,
No Halloween dreams,
No hay rides, no cider,
No costumes, no screams.
The gourds have all gone rotten,
A mushy, soft, flat batch.
Nothing left
But pumpkin dung,
And seeds for
Next years patch.

Growing Up Fast

Polly wanted gifts galore.
She had one birthday; needed more.
She decided her birthday would be every day
And three months later, she passed away.

117

The Silliest Chair Ever

It sits in the corner
At the top of the stairs.
It holds coats and hats
That nobody wears.
When the cat jumps on,
It wobbles and creaks.
No one sits there,
Sometimes for weeks.
It's not very handsome.
It's posture is poor.
There are no others
At the furniture store.
It's rickety and old,
Not useful at all,
And that's why it sits
In the upstairs hall.

Seedle Up

If I could be a beetle,
I'd be big not leetle.
Black on top and red in the meedle,
Ride me if you have a seedle.

Please, Not Stu

I will need someone to help me
With a job I have to do.
It won't take long, or be that hard,
All I ask is, "Please not Stu!"
Stu works very slow and always complains
About working too long and small, little pains.
He likes to rest and take long breaks.
To work with Stu would be a mistake.
If Eddie is ready, I'll work with him.
What's that? He's not? Then send me Jim.
Jim is sick? Then give me Sandy.
She works hard, and her work is dandy.
Sandy won't be here? Sandy is sick?
Is anyone here? What about Nick?
Or Bob or Earl or Kenny or Gary?
Carol or Norman? Tina or Harry?
Everyone is gone? No one is here?
Someone to help me had better appear!
Oh! Hi Stu. How are you?
I was just leaving with work to do.
Do I need any help? No, not this time.
I'll do it myself and be just fine.

121

Genius

Do you know my favorite color?
Do you know how much I weigh?
Do you know my Aunt Matilda's
Favorite game to play?
Do you know where I hide my money?
Do you know my favorite song?
Do you know my favorite breakfast food?
Does my doorbell ding or dong?
Why do I sleep on my stomach?
When do I go to bed?
How do I like my hot-dogs cooked?
Where is the mole on my head?
Who is the person I like the most?
What is my middle name?
Do you know how many books I own?
Is my hamster mean or tame?
Do you know how many pillows
I sleep with every night?
Where is my special hiding place?
Am I afraid of heights?
Do I cry when bugs die?
Who do I hug each day?

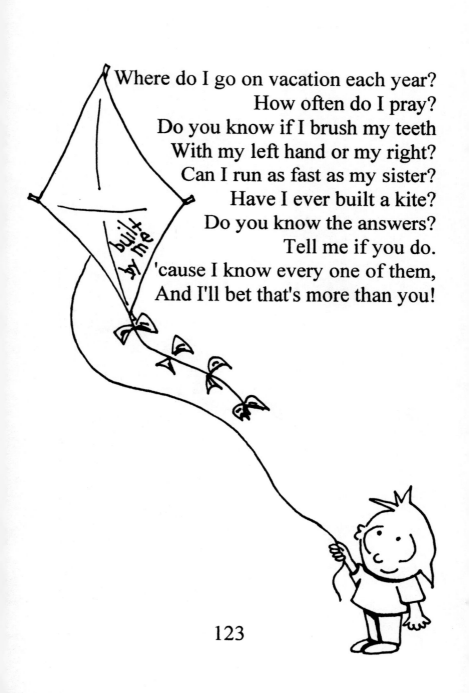

Where do I go on vacation each year?
How often do I pray?
Do you know if I brush my teeth
With my left hand or my right?
Can I run as fast as my sister?
Have I ever built a kite?
Do you know the answers?
Tell me if you do.
'cause I know every one of them,
And I'll bet that's more than you!

built by me

123

Hockey

Slap shot, wrist shot
Line of blue
Red line, off sides
Skates, not shoes
Sticks and pucks
Frozen ice
Goals with nets
Three blind mice
Power plays
Ugly fights
Cheering crowds
Flashing lights
Jerseys, gloves
Pants with pads
Screaming moms
Shouting dads
Penalty box
Plexiglass
Home team, icing
Helmets, masks

Bermuda Shorts

I bought a pair,
And as I feared,
I put them on,
And disappeared.

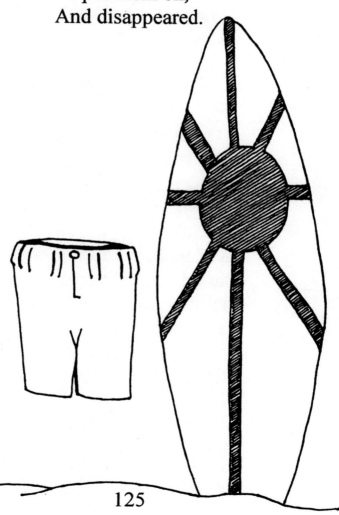

Arcade

Bing! Bang! Boing!
My stomach is churning!
Flash! Crash! Smash!
My eyes are burning!
Click! Click! Click!
My fingers are cramping!
Boom! Bash! Boom!
My feet are stamping!
Pow! Squeal! Squeak!
My ears are ringing!
Ding! Dong! Ring!
My brain is zinging!
Swish! Plop! Grunt!
My back is aching!
Grind! Grind! Groan!
My neck is breaking!
Stamp! Stomp! Scream!
I'm starting to sweat!
Shoot! Clang! Crunch!
My palms are wet!
Clack! Poof! Smack!
I have to move on!
Rats! Rats! Rats!
My quarters are gone!

The Rock

I threw a rock into the air.
If it came down, I don't know where.
What if it hits a kid on the head
And he falls to the ground
And looks like he's dead?
What if a doctor,
Just in time,
Saves his life
And says, "He's fine."?
What if he tells where the rock came from
And that it made his head feel numb?
And what if the police come to the place
Where the rock was hurled into space?
And what if that spot is in front of my home
And they find me there, standing alone?
What if they arrest me and put me in jail
And call my parents to post my bail?
And they say, "No, we cannot go!"
And they leave me in jail for a year or so!
Now that I think, it'll be rare,
If I throw another rock in the air.

Return Policy

I bought a plastic picnic table
And left it in the sun.
My brand new, plastic, picnic table
Melted and started to run.
I took the plastic, gooey mess
Back to the table store.
I complained to the lady who met me there,
That it was a table no more.
She replaced it with
A wooden one,
I took it to
My town.
I put
It next
To the
Fire pit,
And
Promptly
Burned
It down.

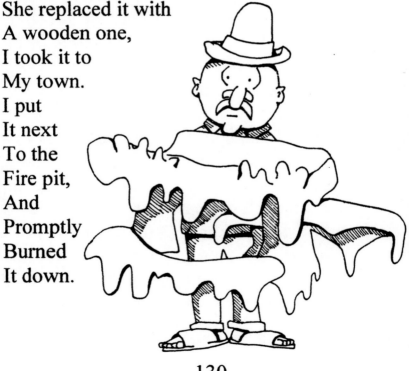

Astronomy

Samuel Moonbeam Lunar McCune,
Alias, Mister Man in the Moon!
Lives in a crater thirty feet deep.
Gets up when you go to sleep.
Takes moon dust from giant jars.
Adds the twinkle to the stars.

131

Rebel

Desk has graffiti?
I drew it!
Dissect a frog?
Won't do it!
Eat school lunch?
Can't chew it!
Film in health?
Won't view it!
Playground whistle?
You blew it!
I'm in trouble?
I knew it!
Sending me home?
Get to it!

133

Trivia Answers

Madagascar
French Revolution
Plutonium alloy
Constitution
Pacific Ocean
San Francisco
Ronald Reagan
Beef burrito
1718
43
Alabama
Redwood tree

Success

Wendy makes the candle.
Calleigh makes the wick.
Love gives us the fire,
And that's what does the trick.

Art

I can turn the wind into a breeze.
I can turn a cough into a sneeze.
I can turn ankles into knees,
But in school, I feel like a crumb.
I can turn bushes into trees.
I can turn mosquitoes into fleas.
I can turn oceans into seas,
But homework makes my head numb.
I can turn carrots into peas.
I can turn you's into me's.
I can turn stress into ease,
But my grades, at times, seem dumb.

A Child's Christmas Carol

Oh, Christmas tree!
Oh, Christmas tree!
How many presents are for me?
Oh, Christmas tree!
Oh, Christmas tree!
I'll take them all, give them to me!
No time for friends, this time of year.
Just give me gifts, no Christmas cheer.
Oh, Christmas tree!
Be good to me!
Or I'll chop you down
And dispose of thee!

A Mother's Christmas Carol

Oh, Christmas tree!
Oh, Christmas tree!
Forgive my son, he's only three.
Oh, Christmas tree!
Oh, Christmas tree!
When he is older, he will see.
That Christmas means, so many things.
It's unimportant, what it brings.
Oh, Christmas tree!
Soon you will see.
My little boy
Won't be greedy.

Walks

Sometimes I walk
Through the cemetery.
It's peaceful and calm,
Not frightening or scary.
I'm not afraid
Of spooks and ghosts.
It's heights and broccoli
That scare me the most.
I stop and visit Mr. Nells
And Mrs. Bucket and Mr. Wells.
I brush leaves off the shaded stones.
I prop up flowers and head for home.
I wonder if the people there
Know I come or if they care.
Either way, I'll do it for me.
Take my walks in the cemetery.

Spirits of the Fourth

Long imprisoned
Hardened case
Shot at night
Into space
Fiery blast
Colorful spray
Free at last
Float away
Over chairs
Smoky flow
Silent wisps
Deafening show
Escaping off
Into the night
Carried far
Out of sight
Dangling limbs?
Tightened ball?
Wanting to leave
No noise at all
Hoping to dance
In a peaceful sky
Far from the noise
Fourth of July

The Eyes Have It

I could not read the chalkboard
At my school today.
I asked the teacher if I could sit closer,
She sat me further away.
She rudely turned her back on me
And wrote something on the board.
"Free ice cream at lunch today!"
I jumped from my seat and roared.
"That is right," my teacher said.
"You can read every word I've written.
Now sit back down in your chair my dear
And try paying closer attention."

145

146

Challenging the Throne

I'm a magician!
I can see visions!
I can control the world!
I'm a sorcerer!
A conqueror!
Watch as my might is unfurled!
I answer to no one!
Do what must be done!
Regardless of who gets hurt!
I fight for right
With all of my might!
I'm wide awake and alert!
I'm invincible and strong!
I can do no wrong!
Look and be filled with dread!
Oh no! It's dad!
And, boy he looks mad!
I better get back into bed!

Elton

Elton died
And I sat and cried.
I did not like
The hurt inside.
I used to sit
And think of him
And tears would come
To my eyes again.
I'm older now,
And it took a while,
But now I can sit,
And think,
And smile.

Bowling Shoes

Bowling shoes
Blue and red
Size? Too big
No grip. No tread
Stinky outside
Stinky in
Two bucks to rent
Podiatric sin

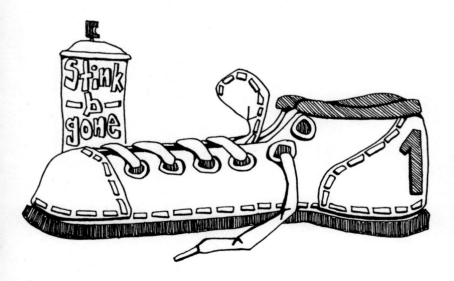

Leave

Who has broken the seal of safety
On the door of hurt and doom?
Who has found my hide out?
Who is looking in my room?
Please give me just a second
To lock away my smiles,
To hang up my hopes and fold my dreams
And put my wishes back into piles.
All I needed was a little break
From your mindless, hopeless place,
A minute or two to catch my breath,
To have my own quiet space.
A space without soccer or homework,
No moms or dads or school,
No drugs or gangs or TV shows
And no one to call me a fool.

Eiriarpnus

Not very big, not very mean
Not very loud, not very clean
Has no hair, two feet tall
Eyes are yellow, teeth are small
Creaky bones, pointed nose
Crooked fingers, crooked toes
Eludes your eyes, much too sly
Much too clever, much too shy
Makes the sounds, in the trees
Midnight steps, morning breeze
Snapping branch, crunching snow
Rolling river as it flows
Distant voice, dripping rain
Falling leaves, whooping crane
In the woods, be aware
Unseen presence, piercing stare.

Wheelbarrow

Wheelbarrow, wheelbarrow, carry my stuff.
Wheelbarrow, wheelbarrow, have enough?
Two scoops of dirt and one of sand.
Wheelbarrow, wheelbarrow, give me a hand.
I want to build a mountain up to the sky.
Together we can do it, just you and I.
I'll fill you up and push you away,
10, 20, 30 or more times a day.
Each time we take a load up our hill,
It'll get bigger and bigger and then, bigger still.
And when our mountain is the biggest and best,
We'll sit up on top for a well deserved rest!

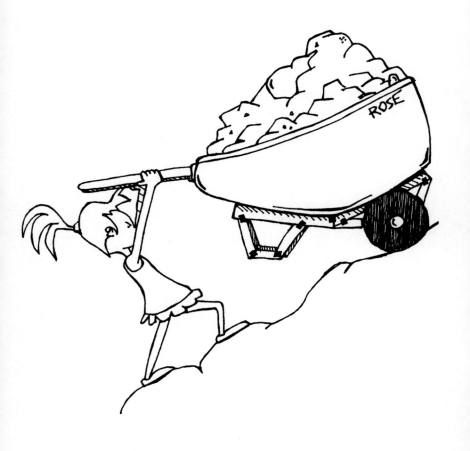

153

Mr. Mister

Mr. Simmer cooks my stews.
Mr. Shoemaker makes my shoes.
Mr. Matz wipes my feet.
Mr. Butcher cuts my meat.
Mr. Farmer grows my fruit.
Mr. Taylor makes my suit.
Mr. Lake gives me water.
Mr. Learner teaches my daughter.
Mr. Armstrong lifts my weights.
Mr. Fisher hooks my baits.
Mr. Hives watches my bees.
Mr. Forrest grows my trees.
Mr. Sweeper cleans my flues.
Mr. Wall blocks my views.

156

Underneath a Semi

Driving along the freeway
Just outside Chicago,
I saw underneath a semi
When I looked outside the window.
I saw a big, spare tire
And a greasy, hanging chain.
Beyond the truck, just my luck,
I saw a passing train.
As I watched and counted the engines
That pulled the train along,
I ran into another car.
I guess I looked too long.

Poor Turtles

I'm glad I'm not a turtle.
I think my back would crack.
If I ever had to carry
My house up on my back.

The Only One Right

200 people told me
That what I thought was wrong.
I told them to be patient
And soon they'd sing my song.
100 people told me
That I wasn't right.
I told them not to worry,
Soon they'd gain their sight.
50 people told me
That what I thought was wrong
I told them, like the others,
That soon they'd come along.
20 people told me
That my thoughts were incorrect.
"I'll have to disagree with you."
I told them quite direct.
One last person told me
That my thoughts could use a turn.
I smiled inside and politely said,
"Someday you will learn."

160

Year in Review

By the time the Halloween candy is gone,
    Thanksgiving has begun.
When the turkey is out of the 'fridge,
    It's time for Christmas fun!
When the presents have all been opened
    And stuck away in rooms,
A brand new year has arrived at night
    With parties filled with booms!
When the party mess is gone,
    It is almost Valentines Day.
When your broken heart has healed,
    It is the Fifth of May!
After the pinata fiesta,
    School has come to a close.
The Fourth of July has snuck up quick
    With wonderful, skylight shows!
After all the smoke has cleared,
    School is straight ahead.
Stuck again, with science and gym,
    And equations in your head.
Quietly, as you sit in school,
    Fall is creeping near.
Time to find another costume,
    And get more treats this year!

Contradiction

I still remember the first time
My father came and said,
"Never look at the sun my son
With the eyes you have in your head.
It will burn your eyes quite badly
If you stare at it too long.
Do not look at the sun at all.
Its burning rays are strong."
For years I've done what I was told,
So many years ago.
I do not stare at the ball in the sky
That gives off heat and glows.
The thing that puzzles me today
Is why my father let
Me go out on summer nights,
And watch the same sun set.

162

Joker, Joker

Joker, Joker why are you
The only one who numbers two?
The number two is not like you.
It numbers four, that's double you.
The three, four, five, six, seven and eight
All number four and think it's great.
The nine, ten, Jack, the King and Queen,
They number four and think it's keen.
Higher than all, in its proper place,
There is also four of the mighty Ace.
So, Joker, Joker why are you
The only one who numbers two?

163

Rocking Horse

Rocking horse!
Rocking horse!
I wish you were a walking horse!
A running horse!
A rodeo horse!
A jumping, bucking, bronco horse!
Rocking horse!
Rocking horse!
I wish you were a talking horse!
A laughing horse!
A singing horse!
A happy voice a'ringing horse!
Rocking horse!
Rocking horse!
Then we could ride away of course!
And eat pies and cakes!
And chocolate shakes!
And talk about all the journeys we'll take!

Anna Belle Hanabelle

Anna Belle Hanabelle
And her tall animal,
Met a small cannibal
At Montreal Falls.
"Are you going to eat me?"
Anna asked sweetly.
He said, "Completely!"
At Montreal Falls.
Her animal heard
The cannibal's word,

166

And anger stirred
At Montreal Falls.
Her angry tall animal
Kicked the small cannibal
(That's understandable)
Over Montreal Falls.
Anna Belle Hanabelle
Thanked her tall animal,
And they never went back
To Montreal Falls.

168

The Purple Sleeping Bag Monster

Out in the desert, Anza Borrego,
Kinda' northeast of north San Diego,
A tale is told of horror and woe.
The purple sleeping bag monster.
Crammed in a tent, a dad and two brothers,
Out on a trip without the boy's mother,
Fussing and twitching and kicking each other.
The purple sleeping bag monster.
High in the rocks, a specter stood.
Dark eyes glared from under a hood.
Noises were heard, but not understood.
The purple sleeping bag monster.
A scratch outside our canvas room!
Someone, I fear, will be consumed!
My bag is purple!! Oh no!! I'm doomed!!
The purple sleeping bag monster!

The Reanimated Remains of Smoky the Flea Ridden Squirrel

Beware! I've seen it! It's hideous and sick!
It's stinky and hairy and covered with ticks!
The once dead remains of Smoky the squirrel,
Brought back to life by a neighborhood girl.
She hooked the corpse up to an old generator,
Gave him a shock, REANIMATOR!
Now he jumps from tree to wire
And dances a jig through a leaf pile fire!
He never sleeps or drinks or eats!
He chases cars that pass in the streets!
I've seen him fall and bang his head,
But nothing can hurt him! He's already dead!
Matted clumps of fur leave a trail
Behind what's left of his bushy tail!

Badfish Creek

19 pieces of moldy bread
Floating through the land of the dead
Past the bones and skulls and dark
Past a dog that cannot bark
Past the hate and hopelessness
Looking for their happiness
They bob and soak, day and night
Always keeping hope in sight
Determined not to fall apart
Sticking together, crust to heart

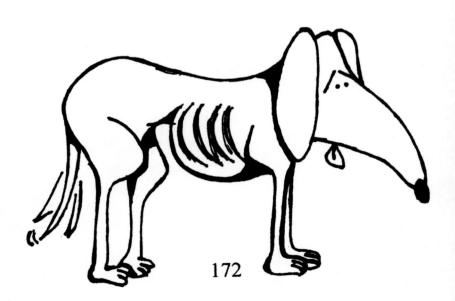

Tweaked

A dog that doesn't bite
A sun that doesn't burn
Fruit that doesn't taste like fruit
Math not hard to learn
The flu the day of the test
Teeth that brush themselves
A hot, gray sidewalk after swimming
Christmas Eve with elves

OOTTAT

OOTTAT, OOTTAT
Sunday afternoon
Dad and me
In jeans and tees
Strolling down the street
OOTTAT, OOTTAT
A summer day in June
We go in
With sleeveless men
Dad sits down in a seat
OOTTAT, OOTTAT
Dad picks a cool cartoon
On his left arm
They do the harm
I watch and think it's neat
OOTTAT, OOTTAT
We'll be leaving soon
With bandage in place
And a smiling face
Back out in the summer heat

174

176

Thanks to...

Kirstin Yorkool
Jim and Linda Gratepairince
Shirley Bestprin-Ciple
All the Wildcats at Westside
Renee Fruntdis-Play
PAC
Bria
Judkins
Uncle Rico
Tom the Preacher Dude

A special thank you to my wife Cheryl who has supported me and my hectic schedule from cover to cover.
143

All the Poems

A

B

C

181

N

O

P

Q

Quit looking, no Q's

R

S

T

Y

You won't find one.

ZZZZZ

Tomorrow is another day. Goodnight.

Oddballs

50/50, 16
@#*!!, 48
$1.00 a Jump!!, 88
180 Degrees, 100

DO A
PIRATE
DANCE